GARY CHAPMAN & JEN MICKELBOROUGH

FAMILY TIME

SIMPLE WAYS TO SPEAK THE 5 LOVE LANGUAGES® TO YOUR KIDS

NORTHFIELD PUBLISHIN

CHICAGO

T0002056

© 2023 by
GARY D. CHAPMAN AND JEN MICKELBOROUGH

Edited by Elizabeth Cody Newenhuyse
Interior and cover design: Erik M. Peterson
Cover and interior illustrations by Jen Mickelborough

Library of Congress Cataloging-in-Publication Data

Names: Chapman, Gary D., 1938- author. | Mickelborough, Jen, author.
Title: Family time : simple ways to speak the 5 love languages to your kids
  / Gary Chapman and Jen Mickelborough.
Description: Chicago : Northfield Publishing, [2023] | Includes index. |
  Summary: "Based on Chapman's best-selling The Five Love Languages®-an
  intentional resource for adding love, meaning, and adventure to your
  family days! Family Time, borne out of the authors own experiences and
  desires to love their children well, is an invaluable resource of
  activities incorporating each of the five love languages"-- Provided by
  publisher.
Identifiers: LCCN 2022046182 (print) | LCCN 2022046183 (ebook) | ISBN
  9780802429711 | ISBN 9780802473486 (ebook)
Subjects: LCSH: Children. | Families. | Love. | BISAC: FAMILY &
  RELATIONSHIPS / General | FAMILY & RELATIONSHIPS / Parenting / General
Classification: LCC HQ767.8 .C445 2023 (print) | LCC HQ767.8 (ebook) |
  DDC 646.7/8--dc23/eng/20220930
LC record available at https://lccn.loc.gov/2022046182
LC ebook record available at https://lccn.loc.gov/2022046183

We hope you enjoy this book from Northfield Publishing. Our goal is to provide high-quality, thought-provoking books and products that connect truth to your real needs and challenges. For more information on other books and products that will help you with all your important relationships, go to www.northfieldpublishing.com or write to:

Northfield Publishing
820 N. LaSalle Boulevard
Chicago, IL 60610

1 3 5 7 9 10 8 6 4 2

Printed in the United States of America

*For my Mum, who took us on adventures
and filled us with appreciation for the
great outdoors, and my Dad, who
built the best bonfires and rope swings.*

—Jen

CONTENTS

INTRODUCTION

By Jen Mickelborough

The time of life while you have young children is busy. Not only are you dealing with the constantly evolving needs of your kids; there's also a lack of sleep, balancing work with family time, and all the events and other hurdles life brings your way. It can be a hectic and exhausting stage of life, and often when you reach your days off it might be the hardest thing to come up with meaningful family activities or ideas of something new to try.

That's certainly what we've experienced in our family life—we are really committed parents, we love our kids wholeheartedly, we try to learn new parenting ideas from books and elsewhere—but we inevitably have gaps in our skills and understanding. We can reach a weekend thinking, "We'd just like a day off, please," when the reality is we have two gorgeous young humans just hoping and waiting for an awesome time with their parents!

We can also find that despite our best efforts and all that we do for our kids, their needs can go unmet, and we're faced with grumpy, dissatisfied kids at the crunch points of the day. Ever tried getting a resistant four-year-old out the door on time when no pair of shoes is acceptable to their tastes? Or cooked a dinner you think your child will love, only for them to reach the table, pull a grimace, and slump off to the sofa and refuse to talk to you? As we faced the reality of our beautiful little humans expressing their displeasure, it occurred to us—maybe we're not loving them in the way that they need!

And so this book is born out of our own experiences and needs—because, though I am familiar with the five love languages, I found it hard to think of new and varied ways to express them to my children—or even what expressing the specific languages I am less attuned to might look like. When you add in fatigue and busy lives, the reality is that, despite good intentions, I was short on ideas and inspiration.

What exactly does it look like to love your child through acts of service? How can I think of a new way to have quality time with my child?

This book is a resource of whole-family activity ideas, with ways to hit each of the five love languages for every activity. So now you can turn family film night into an opportunity to make your kids feel loved as well as be able to relax together. You can know that when you go out for a walk it can become an experience that will fill your kids' hearts with love and wonder for the world around them. There are ideas for wet days and sunny days, ways to relax or to be active, ways to be creative or take in new experiences together. We've included everyday routines of family life, like grocery shopping or leaving the house, and also the bigger rhythms of life that mark the passing of the year and celebrate significant events. If you need an idea in a hurry, use the chart in the Index to scan through for the type of activity you're looking for.

I hope this resource brings ease and enjoyment to your family times, and helps activate all of the five love languages in your household.

A GUIDE TO
THE FIVE LOVE LANGUAGES

By Gary Chapman

Perhaps you have read the original book, *The 5 Love Languages® of Children: The Secret to Loving Children Effectively*, and are familiar with the five love languages. If not, here is the basic concept and a brief description of the love languages.

The question is not: "Do you love your children?" The question is: "Do your children feel loved?" Almost everyone agrees that one of a child's deepest emotional needs is to feel loved. I like to picture that inside every child is an emotional "love tank." If the love tank is full, the child tends to grow up emotionally healthy. If the tank is empty, the child grows up with many internal emotional struggles, and in the teenage years will likely go looking for love elsewhere, often in the wrong places.

In my counseling, I discovered that what makes one child feel loved does not make another child feel loved. My research discovered five basic ways to express love to children. I call them the five love languages. Each child has a primary love language which speaks most deeply to them emotionally. If parents do not discover and speak their primary love language, they will not feel loved, even if the parents are speaking some of the other languages.

Most parents genuinely love their children, but not all children feel loved. A thirteen-year-old young man ran away from home and ended up in my office. He said to me, "My parents don't love me. They love my brother, but they don't love me." I knew his parents and I knew that they loved him. The problem was they had never learned to speak his primary love language. So here is a brief description of the five love languages.

PHYSICAL TOUCH—affirming touch says "I love you" to this child. When the child is little, parents hold and cuddle their baby. As the child gets older, they hold them on their laps. Appropriate hugs, kisses, and high fives all communicate love.

WORDS OF AFFIRMATION—using words to express appreciation. "You did a great job cleaning your room." "One of the things I appreciate about you is . . ." "Your hair looks beautiful." The words may focus on the child's appearance, personality trait, or behavior.

QUALITY TIME—giving the child your undivided attention. Depending on the age and interest of the child, this may be playing games together, discussing a book or movie, or taking a walk together. The important thing is that they have your full attention. If you are talking with the child and your phone rings, let it go to voice mail, thus demonstrating that the child is more important than anyone on the phone.

RECEIVING GIFTS—a tangible token that you were thinking about them. If you go on a business trip, or to the grocery store, bring them a surprise. The gifts need not be expensive. It's the thought that counts. If Receiving Gifts is their primary love language, then gifts speak loudly of your love.

ACTS OF SERVICE—doing something for the child that you know they would like for you to do. Helping with homework, mending a doll dress, fixing their bicycle, or playing basketball in the backyard all speak love to the child whose love language is Acts of Service. The old saying "Actions speak louder than words" is true for this child.

Three questions will help you discover the child's primary love language:

1. How does the child normally relate to you and other family members? Typically, the child will speak their own love language to others.

2. What does your child complain about? The complaint reveals the love language.

3. What request does the child make most often? They are requesting what would make them feel loved.

I would also encourage you to visit 5lovelanguages.com and take the love languages quiz for kids—there's one quiz for eight-year-olds and younger and one for nine- to twelve-year-olds.

Don't hear me saying that you should only speak the child's primary love language. We give heavy doses of their primary language, but we also speak the other four, because we want the child to learn how to receive and give love in all five languages. This leads to strong emotional health. However, if we don't focus on the primary love language, the child will not feel loved. The purpose of this book is to give you illustrated ideas on how to speak each of the child's love languages.

MOVIE NIGHT

Indoor

Turn this relaxing family time into an opportunity to speak all five love languages to your children. For some families this might become an end-of-week tradition that makes a relaxing and fun start to the weekend. For others it might be a special occasion, reward, or treat. You could make your child a plate of sandwiches to eat during the film and give yourself a night off from cooking a family meal.

PHYSICAL TOUCH—Snuggle up on the sofa, grab a soft blanket, or build a cushion fort to watch from.

WORDS OF AFFIRMATION—Ask your child what they liked about the movie—listen to and affirm their opinions and experiences.

QUALITY TIME—Be fully present for the film with no other distractions. Take your child on a special trip to the store first to buy popcorn for the evening.

RECEIVING GIFTS—Pick up some treats they love. Buy or rent a new film they'd love to see.

ACTS OF SERVICE—Make time to set up the room together with your child the way they like it to be. Give them the best spot for viewing.

FAMILY OLYMPICS
Indoor, Outdoor, Physical

A great opportunity for fun, teamwork, and encouragement is to run your own family Olympics. On wet days make indoor game variations; if it's nice outside, then head to the park or set up in your yard. Ideas to try: beanbag toss, three-legged race, egg-and-spoon race, sack race, or follow a trail balancing a beanbag on your head. Kids can have fun thinking up ways to make races harder for the faster family members—think of it as a mini "Yes Day" and be prepared to do some silly things; then watch the giggles as you indulge your kids' sense of fun.

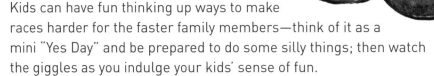

PHYSICAL TOUCH—Be sure to include touch activities—wrestling, three-legged race, piggyback rides, leapfrog, wheelbarrow race. This is a great opportunity for your kid to help and assist other family members.

WORDS OF AFFIRMATION—Praise your child's efforts, skills, and ideas. Be on the lookout for things you can affirm. Winning isn't the goal; encouragement and affirmation are.

QUALITY TIME—Prepare and participate in the challenges together, devoting your full attention to the activities.

RECEIVING GIFTS—Buy or make the equipment to compete: beanbags made from a pair of socks and dried beans, or blindfolds made from some fabric or an old t-shirt. Present them in a "mystery box" to introduce the idea. Get the kids to make winners' certificates, trophies, or rosettes.

ACTS OF SERVICE—Help your child choose an outfit. Prepare the events together. Make a halftime snack like orange slices.

BIRTHDAYS

Seasons & Celebrations

Birthdays are an obvious time to celebrate your child—here are some ideas for expressing all of the five love languages on their special day. Families create their own customs for birthdays, like a special breakfast or dinner on the day, choosing a family activity, taking time to look back on the past year's ups and downs, and looking forward to the next year with hopes and dreams.

PHYSICAL TOUCH—Make wake-up snuggles in bed a birthday ritual for little ones. Present older kids with a voucher to get a back scratch or massage from you.

WORDS OF AFFIRMATION—In their birthday card write all their great qualities that you see and admire. Tell them how much you love them and are proud of them, and ways you've seen them grow this year. Help them write thank-you notes or call to express thanks to people who've given them gifts or helped them in some way this year.

QUALITY TIME—Go on a special activity or birthday date of their choosing together.

RECEIVING GIFTS—Kids don't need lots of presents, or expensive ones—most important is to know they are being cherished and celebrated as their gift is given.

ACTS OF SERVICE—Plan a special meal or party. Set up balloons or bunting in their room while they sleep or to be waiting for them at the dining table for breakfast time.

DRAW YOUR OWN PORTRAITS

Indoor, Creative

You do NOT need to be a skilled artist to do this—in fact, less realistic drawings often hold more charm (just think of all those pictures your kid makes). Why not draw or paint with your nondominant hand to take the pressure off and enjoy your silly side, or use nonrealistic colors for your portraits. You might just end up with something to put on the wall that reminds you of some special family times as you draw each other's portraits.

PHYSICAL TOUCH—Touch and stroke your child's face and hair as you observe their features.

WORDS OF AFFIRMATION—Tell your child all the unique and special things you observe in their physique. When you comment on their creation, try to make nonqualifying observations—"I see you used a bold line for my eyes." "The green for my cheeks is really interesting."

QUALITY TIME—Clear your schedule so nothing can interrupt your time together, make eye contact, and chat with your child as you sit and create.

RECEIVING GIFTS—Find some new art and craft supplies, and wrap them up before you start. Find frames for your creations and present the framed pieces before they go up on the walls for all to see.

ACTS OF SERVICE—Set the mood with some background music, and prepare the space so you don't need to worry about any mess your child makes. Ask your child if they'd like to help with setup or tidy-up.

NATURE EXPLORER
Outdoor, Physical

Taking in somewhere new or seeing a familiar place through fresh explorer eyes is a great bonding experience. Be sure to turn over rocks to find bugs, look above at the clouds or tree canopy, and get up close to the things your child is drawn to. Kids are way more engaged on a walk if they have a mission—find a flower in every color of the rainbow, see how many different leaf shapes you can find, imagine creatures who might live in different places you pass, or dream about a great adventure you could have in this environment.

PHYSICAL TOUCH—Hold hands while you walk or give them a shoulder ride. Help them climb trees and rocks or logs. Get them to help each other (or you!) on tricky paths.

WORDS OF AFFIRMATION—Affirm their discoveries: be curious about what they notice and speak it back to them. Notice and praise them when they give words of affirmation to other family members.

QUALITY TIME—Give them your full attention, put your phone on "Do Not Disturb," and even take no photos—just fill your heart with mental snapshots of your time together.

RECEIVING GIFTS—Set up an explorer bag with snacks, a pad and pencil, or a spyglass/binoculars. Give them a collecting bag to store up treasures they find.

ACTS OF SERVICE—Carry their bag or coat when they get tired of being loaded down. Prepare a snack and drinks for a picnic stop en route.

URBAN WALK
Outdoor, Creative, Physical

When you're in an urban landscape you can always see more when you go out intentionally looking past your everyday routines. Give your kids a task like finding every number from 0 to 10 in order, or find every letter of the alphabet. You could take crayons and do rubbings of manhole covers or other interesting textures. Look above ground level and see what you can spot above shops and doorways, or get kid-level with your surroundings and look at the tiny landscapes in front of your noses.

There's a reason kids get stuck staring at stuff—what's around you can be fascinating when you stop and really look.

PHYSICAL TOUCH—Scrunch down in the dirt next to your kid, put your arm around them as you stare up at buildings, or carry them on your shoulders if they get tired.

WORDS OF AFFIRMATION—Make sure you really listen to what your child sees, reflect back to them what they're saying, and ask them questions about their observations.

QUALITY TIME—This activity doesn't have to take all day, but your undivided attention and involvement in this activity will speak volumes to your child.

RECEIVING GIFTS—Present your child with a little detective's notebook and pencil for their observations. Or a collecting bag to gather any treasures they find. Pack a treat you can share when you need a rest and present it as a surprise.

ACTS OF SERVICE—Help your child prepare for your walk by finding the right clothes and shoes or maybe finding a bag for anything they want to collect.

PLAYGROUND ADVENTURES
Outdoor, Physical

Find a new park to visit—try a new area of your city or visit a nearby town; find somewhere away from your regular spots. Ask friends where they go to get local tips, or try online maps or a trip advice website and check the family fun section.

PHYSICAL TOUCH—Hold hands or give your child a piggyback or shoulder ride as you explore. Help them climb new playground equipment or scale a tree.

WORDS OF AFFIRMATION—Ask them what they think of the new location—likes and dislikes. Listen to and affirm their opinions and see what it teaches you about their interests.

QUALITY TIME—Get down on their level and join in with their exploration. Be the parent who joins in with their kid regardless of who's watching.

RECEIVING GIFTS—Buy and wrap a ball, Frisbee, or kite to play with on your trip. Visit a café and let them choose a treat.

ACTS OF SERVICE—Let them be the leader. Follow their instincts of where and what they want to explore. Assist them by looking at a map on your device or information about a certain place.

COFFEES & CHALKS
Outdoor, Creative, Physical

Take a family date to a local coffee shop where there's a nearby park or stretch of concrete to get creative with a box of sidewalk chalk. Buy yourselves takeout drinks and then head out to create mythical creatures together as you draw, write life-affirming messages for passersby, or invent a chalked trail that you and others can enjoy with pathways, shapes to leap between, or stepping-stones to tiptoe along.

PHYSICAL TOUCH—Make physical connection part of your play. Scooch down side by side as you draw, or make some tricky parts to your trail that you have to carry or assist your child over.

WORDS OF AFFIRMATION—Affirm the ideas they have, ask their opinion as you create, and praise the effort they are putting in. Leave positive messages for the people who'll encounter your creations.

QUALITY TIME—You can make this activity last as long as you want! Not only will you be filling up your kids' love tank, but you'll also be leaving a Quality Time gift for the people who follow you.

RECEIVING GIFTS—Keep the chalks a secret! Wrap them up to present to your child once you're out.

ACTS OF SERVICE—Help them achieve their idea—get down and chalky with them.

FAMILY MASTERPIECE

Indoor, Creative

The results of this activity don't matter so much as the time spent together creating a piece of art. Enjoy spending time collaborating and observing the ideas your kids have. For supplies, buy a canvas board to work on or alternatively use some delivery box cardboard. Grab any of these: paints, crayons, pencils, felt tips, patterned paper, tissue paper, glues, glitter, and sequins. Top tip—if the results are important to you, provide supplies in similar colors to avoid a mud-puddle result!

PHYSICAL TOUCH—Get messy together—do handprints and finger painting, and work shoulder to shoulder.

WORDS OF AFFIRMATION—Take notice of their choices and describe what you see them doing or how they work together. You'll notice as you model this that they'll also do it back to you.

QUALITY TIME—Connect over the choices they've made, or if they're feeling unsure what to do, take time to ask them about their preferences of color or materials and encourage them to trust their instincts.

RECEIVING GIFTS—Wrap up or box up the art supplies to be opened at the start of your activity. You could use the resulting artwork to make a gift for friends or family members.

ACTS OF SERVICE—Set out the space and supplies together. Offer to tidy-up together, or take one for the team and tidy by yourself (in peace and quiet!).

BAKE-OFF!

Indoor

Are there any kids who don't enjoy baking? Savory or sweet, simple or complex, this is a great activity to enjoy together. Make it a one-off or take turns with different family members each week for the full Bake-Off experience. If you're not sure where to start, buy a baking packet from the supermarket or look up kid- or family-friendly recipes online. Only pick ones with five-star ratings and easy-to-find ingredients. You might even find that by joining with the cooking process your kids will be willing to try some foods they're not normally used to eating.

PHYSICAL TOUCH—Get close as you help beat the mixture, break open the eggs, move heavy bowls, and wipe up the messes—lots of opportunity for side-by-side touches as you help them.

WORDS OF AFFIRMATION—Compliment their work and the time they put into it. Spend time asking them about their taste preferences and choices, listening openly.

QUALITY TIME—Carve out some clear time and set the mood by playing family-favorite music.

RECEIVING GIFTS—Wrap any of these: sprinkles for cake decorations, a wooden spoon with their name on it, an apron, or any other specific supplies for their kitchen creations.

ACTS OF SERVICE—Be available to lend a hand with tricky stages or deciphering recipes. Run cleanup around them as they work so you can all relax at the end of the bake. Allow them to be as hands-on as possible, even if it means more mess gets made. Bake a gift together to give to others.

BATHTIME

Everyday

Daily jobs like these can feel like another chore to get through, but they can also be a chance to connect with your children and speak their love language clearly. Finding ways to eliminate the hurry can really help take the pressure off, so consider changing your schedule so there's leeway for those things that should take one minute but stretch to five before your eyes!

PHYSICAL TOUCH—Undressing, washing, drying, and dressing your child can all be expressions of love through physical touch. Roll your child up in a blanket, give them a silly joggle, and enjoy the resulting giggles.

WORDS OF AFFIRMATION—In a world that creates strong expectations on how we look, bathtime is a great opportunity to build up your child's self-esteem about their appearance. Tell them what you admire about their hair, eyes, skin, body; tell them they have a strong and capable body, talk about the physical things they are good at, and you will give them confidence that grows as their body does.

QUALITY TIME—Find a bathtime "game" that your child enjoys— toy boats that perform rescue missions, foam letters or numbers for some fun stealth learning, experiment playfully with rhyming words together, or create characters with special voices who go on imaginary adventures together.

RECEIVING GIFTS—Buy some bath crayons or a little bath toy for a bathtime surprise.

ACTS OF SERVICE—If your kid finds undressing, washing, drying, or dressing hard work, then take the time to help them and have a moment's connection—doing these things for them won't last forever, so see it as an opportunity to cherish something that they'll be too big for one day!

MEALTIME
Everyday

Having a family mealtime that's free of distraction (i.e., technology) is a great way to connect. If midweek is busy with activities, get creative with a weekend mealtime that works for everyone—take your pick of breakfast, brunch, lunch, or dinner!

PHYSICAL TOUCH—Make time for a hug, either as you gather at the table if you've not connected sooner in the day, or at the end of the meal before you disperse. With older kids you can give a side hug, high five, or shoulder squeeze as you pass them setting or clearing the table.

WORDS OF AFFIRMATION—Affirm and encourage your child as they share about their day, tell them the good qualities you see them growing in, and tell them how much you appreciate who they are.

QUALITY TIME—Take turns talking about the day. Try out "Highs & Lows" or "Lemons & Cherries," where everyone picks something that happened during the day to tell about. If your child enjoys cooking, then this is an easy win for spending time together. They may not last all that long, but five minutes of cutting up vegetables with you could be the highlight of their day.

RECEIVING GIFTS—This one is easy—cook a favorite meal or get in a favorite fruit or dessert. Food is a simple gift. If your child likes helping you cook, take them to buy a suitable stepstool just for them so they know they're welcome in the kitchen with you.

ACTS OF SERVICE—Finish mealtime with a team cleanup; find age-appropriate jobs like clearing plates for little ones or wiping the table. Try loading the dishwasher or washing up as they get older. Have an "all-in policy"—nobody stops until everyone stops.

GROCERIES

Weekly

It might not be your preference to go grocery shopping with small people in tow, but often there just isn't another option. So how can we turn this regular chore into an opportunity to communicate love to our kids? Try some of these ideas . . .

PHYSICAL TOUCH—Pushing a shopping cart around the store presents some great opportunities for physical touch. If your child is younger and they're riding in the cart, you can bend forward to cuddle them as you go around, give them a stroke as you lean past them, or if it's chilly in the store, wrap them up in a scarf or extra layer. If they're walking, let them help steer the cart with you behind them to guide or use gentle touch to navigate obstacles in the store.

WORDS OF AFFIRMATION—Let your child know you like spending time with them and having them along with you. Use this chance to be together to reflect to them something they've done well this week, or tell them something you admire about them.

QUALITY TIME—Give yourself an extra ten minutes so you're not rushing, and take time to go a little slower so you can have a conversation as you go around. If you're not sure what to talk about, start with the food you're seeing and what they like or dislike eating.

RECEIVING GIFTS—Decide ahead of time something your child can choose in the store. Maybe it's the shape of pasta this week or a fruit or vegetable they like, a magazine, or even plan what meal they'd like, and then buy the ingredients together. Plan ahead and you can sidestep the inevitable sugary foods request.

ACTS OF SERVICE—Kids love to be helpful, and you'll top off their Acts of Service tank by giving them a chance to help. They could read the list, push the cart, find certain foods, load the conveyor belt, or carry the bags—plenty of choices!

GETTING DRESSED
Everyday

Why is it that some days kids can dress themselves in no time and with no help, and others it takes forever for nothing to happen?! Just remember that you won't still be dressing them when they're teenagers! For now, here are some options to make the most of this daily requirement . . .

PHYSICAL TOUCH—Dressing is a great opportunity for physical touch, strokes, and squishes as clothes go on, and offer a great big cuddle at the end as a reward once they're fully dressed.

WORDS OF AFFIRMATION—This is a great time to instill some body confidence in your kids. Boys and girls need to hear from their parents that they are strong and capable, that their muscles are good for being active and having fun.

QUALITY TIME—It's choice time! Does this feel like a chore or a chance to connect with your child at the start of the day? Your intention will be felt by your child.

RECEIVING GIFTS—Kids keep on growing, so presenting new clothes as a gift is a great way to add some special connection into this everyday need. (Though think about your timing—do you want them to wear that new item right *this* moment?)

ACTS OF SERVICE—Laundry, laundry, laundry! Let your child know you are loving them by washing their clothes, and invite them to join with you in doing the laundry so they start learning how to do it themselves. Or try putting clean items away together.

LEAVING THE HOUSE
Everyday

Okay, we've all been there—how long can it possibly take to get on a pair of shoes and a coat? Sometimes it feels like forever! There's no doubt that this is a big crunch point for lots of families, so here are some ways to fill up the love tanks and take the edge off a time of the day that can be stressful.

PHYSICAL TOUCH—If your child loves physical touch, then work this into the leaving routine: play "you can't get your foot in this shoe!" and then give their legs a squeeze once each foot is in. Zip up the coat and finish by cupping that beautiful little face in your hands when you get to the top of the zipper. Offer giant squishy hugs for anyone who's fully ready, or a big family sandwich hug once you're all ready to get out the door.

WORDS OF AFFIRMATION—Encourage all those skills of self-reliance and autonomy with every little step they do: "You got to the door!" "You found your shoes, well done!" "You've already got your coat, you're so quick," "You have your bag ready, great remembering." Every positive thing they hear builds their belief in themselves and will help next time. If they've been really helpful getting out the door, let them know how much it helps you out.

QUALITY TIME / ACTS OF SERVICE—Sometimes it might feel like our kids should really be doing more for themselves, but sometimes you have to choose what's worth pushing for and what will make your life easier to do yourself—so if your kid likes to have help getting ready, make this a moment to connect and give your help gladly and generously. It'll be a little moment of quality time in their day that brings connection rather than frustration.

RECEIVING GIFTS—Make a reward chart with your kid for leaving the house, and decide together what treat they'll get for a set amount of good exits. Make sure you're both clear about what a good exit looks like!

BEDTIME
Everyday

Ever noticed how children can come alive just as you're trying to turn out the light at bedtime? With a bit of adjustment you can take advantage of bedtime delaying

tactics, so you're actually filling their love tank. Reconsider your bedtime schedule to allow for these extras so you can stay in the moment with your child, without getting frustrated at the "delays."

PHYSICAL TOUCH—Changing into nightclothes, brushing hair and teeth, bedtime stories, and tuck-ins are all great opportunities for physical touch. Offer different options to see what your kid would most like—it might be that they'd find a story while you snuggle together before bed most special, or it's actually a debrief of the day with a flashlight under a blanket that would fill their love tank.

WORDS OF AFFIRMATION—Tell your child you love them and are proud of them before they go to bed, especially if it's been a day with emotional bumps. Take time to apologize if you've done or said something that upset them, and make sure they know nothing affects how much you love them.

QUALITY TIME—Some kids will suddenly remember all their news from the day just as you're tucking them in and are ready to leave, so make a plan that leaves time for this sudden opportunity for connection and hearing about their world.

RECEIVING GIFTS—Give your child a gift that they will use every night and be reminded of your love—a special cuddly toy, new bedding, a soft blanket, or some fun pajamas.

ACTS OF SERVICE—Work out with your kid what parts of bedtime they find hardest, and make a plan to help them with these things. They'll feel deeply loved by the time you give helping them.

CLEANING & CHORES
Everyday

Do your kids help with chores? One day your small people will be big people looking after themselves, so starting them on chores that suit their age right now is in their future interest! Asking directly is effective—"Could you please help me by bringing those plates over?" Anything that starts with a "Do you want to . . . ?" is way more likely to receive a no!

PHYSICAL TOUCH—Whatever chore you're doing, if you get alongside your kid to demonstrate or do it together, you can give an encouraging squeeze of the arm or pat on the back—any touch that shows you see and appreciate them.

WORDS OF AFFIRMATION—Make sure to express your thanks for their help clearly and directly. Tell them how much you appreciate their effort and how it makes you feel to have help and see them taking responsibility.

QUALITY TIME—Most chores can be done by two people at once, so find something you can do together and work as a team. Being engaged in a task is often a great space to talk and in a more relaxed way. Play some music you both enjoy to make the most of the moment.

RECEIVING GIFTS—Try a pair of gloves the right size for your kid, a fun feather duster, or an apron that's just right for their height.

ACTS OF SERVICE—By working on chores together, you are teaching your kid to look after themselves and how to serve others. You can also work together on your kid's room to teach them the satisfaction of a clean and tidy space. Some kids might not like the idea of tidying their room but actually prefer the cleaning part, so this can be a good way to help them get in the habit.

CLOTHES SHOPPING
Everyday

At some point your small person is going to become an independent big person, and clothes are one of the ways you can encourage them to express themselves as they work out who they are.

PHYSICAL TOUCH—Little ones can be helped with dressing and changing, either trying items on while in the store or checking out new outfits at home. Bigger kids will start to need more privacy, but you can stand with them in front of the mirror and give reassuring and encouraging physical touch as they look at new clothes.

WORDS OF AFFIRMATION—Affirm both how the clothes look on them and also how the choices they're making reflect who they are and what they like to do.

QUALITY TIME—Make sure you have enough time that the shopping isn't rushed, and give your child your full attention while they look and decide what is important to them.

RECEIVING GIFTS—New clothes are a fun gift for most kids. Whether they're new from a store or bought secondhand, they can be presented as a gift and fun occasion.

ACTS OF SERVICE—Serve your child in the way that works best for them when getting new clothes. Some children might be best consulted to meet specific tastes, while others may love surprises and choices, and you can get whatever looks good to you and still meet their satisfaction.

ERRAND BUDDY

Everyday

Here's a way to take the pressure off that "getting everyone out the door" moment and be able to invest your attention on your child. Instead of trying to do things as a group or with friends, go one-on-one with your child. This can still be getting jobs done or incorporating functional things you need to do, but going solo with your child frees up negotiating anyone else's needs, and you can fit in something that is a treat for your child while you're out.

PHYSICAL TOUCH—Show physical affection with a hug or squeeze or stroke as you walk along. If they notice something, stop and stand close together to inspect it—join the moment they're in.

WORDS OF AFFIRMATION—Be overt in telling your child you like spending time with them. Think of something that happened in the last week you can praise them for—an achievement, a way they helped, an action that took courage or perseverance.

QUALITY TIME—This whole activity is quality time as long as you approach it as an activity you do together and put away distractions like phones.

RECEIVING GIFTS—Find a way to incorporate a little gift or treat as you're out: stopping for a hot chocolate, choosing a book or magazine, buying some new stationery.

ACTS OF SERVICE—You could use this moment to do an act of service together for someone who would appreciate it: buying flowers for a friend or picking up groceries for a neighbor.

CHRISTMAS
Seasons & Celebrations

Christmas can be a really busy time of year, with friends and family to see, not to mention decorations and presents. Take time to consider what's really important to you as a family, and make it a priority that those things happen. Try having a family meeting and taking down everyone's top 3 things to do, and use this to make an action list.

PHYSICAL TOUCH—Make sure to show your love with big hugs, affectionate pats, or an arm around your child's shoulders.

WORDS OF AFFIRMATION—As you spend more time with friends and family, make a point of saying complimentary things to your child in the presence of others. It's not showing off; affirming your child's attributes in public is a significant way of honoring who they are.

QUALITY TIME—Make sure you are spending time just as a family, even if it means saying no to some things. Kids will remember the simplest things—decorating cookies, putting up the tree, and watching a Christmas film. Discussing the film with children is a great quality time experience.

RECEIVING GIFTS—Encourage your children to think about gifts they can give to take part in the festivities. It could be a craft they make or a picture they draw.

ACTS OF SERVICE—As a family, take part in a shoebox gift appeal or some other way of giving to those in need, such as supporting a food bank or homeless charity.

EASTER

Creative, Seasons & Celebrations

In whatever way you celebrate Easter as a
family, it's a great opportunity to mark the
season and enjoy family time together. An
Easter hunt is a fun activity, as kids love
finding treasures. The simple fun of a craft
activity is often popular, decorating egg

shapes to adorn your home and letting your child help choose where
their artwork goes up.

PHYSICAL TOUCH—If you have an Easter hunt, hold hands with little
ones as they search or celebrate successes with high fives, or even
go big and throw them up in the air to land in your safe arms!

WORDS OF AFFIRMATION—When doing arts and crafts, comment
on their work without qualifying whether you think it's "good"; try
"look at how you've put that blue and orange side by side" or "I can
see strong lines" or "you're really taking time with those edges."

This gives your child room to keep trying new things rather than having a narrow definition of what's "right."

QUALITY TIME—Make sure your egg hunt will last a suitable amount of time for everyone present, so you can all enjoy the moment without it passing too quickly or dragging on. If you're decorating eggs, get set up in a good space and put on some fun tunes so you can all get absorbed in the moment.

RECEIVING GIFTS—If you want to avoid heaps of chocolate in the house, hide pretend eggs and have a prize ceremony at the end with a little gift for all participants. If you've bought new supplies for crafting, then present these in a little box or bag to be opened as a gift.

ACTS OF SERVICE—Let your child know you're spending time setting up a special activity for them; give them the anticipation of knowing time is being spent preparing for them to have fun later!

VACATIONS AWAY FROM HOME
Seasons & Celebrations

If you're lucky enough to be able to take a break away from home, you can create your own family culture of holiday. Start with what you really enjoy yourself, and invite your kids to join in with your way, as well as adding in their own personal desires.

PHYSICAL TOUCH—When you arrive at your vacation home, explore around the house together. Play hide and seek where the hider gets a big hug when caught, or play "sardines" where one person hides and everyone squishes into the same spot until the last seeker finds them.

WORDS OF AFFIRMATION—At the start of the vacation, take out a sheet of paper and write down three things each person would love to do during your break, and then do everything you can to make them happen. This shows value and respect for everyone's preferences and affirms how each person in your family is made and what they'd like from the vacation. Younger kids can draw pictures to help remember their goals.

QUALITY TIME—Make sure you work time into the day where you get to be one-on-one with your kid. Try to literally get on their level—this might mean lying on the dirt so you can hunt bugs together, but getting fully into their world will help you appreciate how they see life, and they'll feel your full connected presence.

RECEIVING GIFTS—If you have a long journey, buy a little toy that can keep them busy on the way, like a cuddly toy or character toy they can play make-believe with, or find a reading or activity book you can pull out as a surprise gift for that "I'm bored" moment! Encourage your kid to find little treasures for their friends as vacation gifts, or buy a little souvenir for a special person in their life.

ACTS OF SERVICE—Helping your child pack a bag of clothes or toys for a visit is a great way of showing love through acts of service.

VACATIONS AT HOME

Indoor, Seasons & Celebrations

A change from school days to vacation days might come as a welcome relief or feel fraught with extra pressures, especially if your time off work doesn't coincide with your child's. Regardless of where you find yourself, you can create a culture around vacations that suits your family, with your own rituals that create a sense of holiday that works for you all.

PHYSICAL TOUCH—As you talk over the end of school and what vacation will look like, sit close or cuddle with your kid, or have a play fight and wrestle to let off some steam.

WORDS OF AFFIRMATION—Use the break from school to look back and affirm your child in things they have done well or persevered through this year. See if you can be specific about something they've done—a test result, a piece of work, the way they've worked on something challenging, or how things have been going with their friends.

QUALITY TIME—Make time for an activity you wouldn't normally do together. Make it something you do together that marks vacation time as different and special. It could be trying a creative activity, going for a long walk, making time for a library visit, or visiting an attraction.

RECEIVING GIFTS—Mark the start of the vacation with a little treat that suits your kid's interests—art supplies, a book, a new computer game, baking supplies, something related to music or sports . . .

ACTS OF SERVICE—Help your child prepare things they'll enjoy spending time on, whether it's a trip to the library for new books, tidying a desk so there's space to create, or maybe setting up some favorite toys with extra space.

WEEKENDS

Weekly

Weekends offer a change of pace and a chance to create your own rhythm that suits your family needs. Any activity you find that doubles up as rest or recreation for you is extremely worthwhile. It's easy to plan a lot for weekends like catching up on jobs that need doing or people you'd like to see, but it's worth cutting that list and reducing the pressure to get from one thing to the next. Weekends can also offer a bit of space for the things that don't fit in the busyness of the week—getting out paints for some creative time, building a track that covers the kitchen floor, taking a walk and not minding that long detour, or just hanging around in pajamas half the day because there's no need to rush out of the house for school and work.

PHYSICAL TOUCH—Take time to stop and catch up with your kids on the sofa, or get down on the floor and play with them (see how long it takes for someone to climb on top of you!). If you're not in the habit of cuddling, then ask directly, "Would you like a cuddle? Shall we sit together? I'd like to hear about your week."

WORDS OF AFFIRMATION—Take time to comment on the things they've done well this week—getting ready for school, getting homework done, doing something for a sibling. Listen to their desires for the weekend and affirm their needs and choices.

QUALITY TIME—Even if you have lots to get done, make sure you carve out time that's just for you and your child. Ask them what they'd like to do with you with their time, or work together ahead of time to make a list of weekend activities they'd like to do with you so you have a ready-made set of options to choose from.

RECEIVING GIFTS—Find some little treats for the weekend they can utilize in their free time like an activity book or some new pens, or get a special food treat you know they love that adds something extra to the weekend days.

ACTS OF SERVICE—Make the home function well for the weekends. Make space for their activities. If chores need to be done, work together so they're out of the way. Most kids gravitate toward specific home jobs, so find out what they'd like to do and find ways to let them help you in this way (they may not do it perfectly, but if they start now then one day they might!).

ACHIEVEMENTS

Seasons & Celebrations

With the wonderful differences in personality and skills of our kids, what achievement looks like will be varied—doing something brave, working hard at something challenging, showing kindness and empathy, succeeding at academics or sports, or making progress in a hobby. There's much we can choose to celebrate in our children, and marking their achievements is a great way of encouraging growth and hard work.

PHYSICAL TOUCH—Give your child hugs, high fives, a pat on the back, or a hair tousle as you congratulate them. Encourage your child to also congratulate others in this way when they notice an achievement.

WORDS OF AFFIRMATION—Take time to clearly articulate why you are proud of your child: what skills and personal traits are you seeing them work at or grow in?

QUALITY TIME—Stop and be present as you comment on your child's achievement. Take time to look over something they've made thoroughly and ask questions, give your full attention to a repeat performance, or spend time hearing about what they were thinking and feeling.

RECEIVING GIFTS—Have a stash of mini rewards for achievements, or collect "tokens" that build toward a gift of choice.

ACTS OF SERVICE—Help your child prepare for their activity or event, or help them get cleaned up, tidied away, and sorted out afterward.

END OF SCHOOL YEAR
Seasons & Celebrations

The school year represents big stages in your child's life. By marking and celebrating the end of the school year you are teaching them to observe their own progress and achievements and celebrate themselves. It's a chance to look back on what they've done and achieved, or get closure on any harder aspects of the year and clear the way for what will come next.

PHYSICAL TOUCH—Mark the end of the year with a big energy release: have a dance party, fill a room with balloons, have a water gun fight—lots of fun and lots of opportunity for playful physical connection.

WORDS OF AFFIRMATION—Make an end-of-year achievement certificate for your child expressing the ways you've seen them grow and succeed this year. Find a prominent place to put it so they can be reminded of your pride in them.

QUALITY TIME—Have your child choose an activity they love to do with you to mark the end of school, and book time in your calendar to make this happen.

RECEIVING GIFTS—An end-of-term gift could reflect something new they've learned or tried this year, or maybe something that will provide entertainment and activity going into the school holiday.

ACTS OF SERVICE—To mark the end of term, clear away the school uniform and term-time items so there's space for some holiday activities.

BACK TO SCHOOL

Seasons & Celebrations

Going back to school may cause some mixed feelings in your household. Some preparation reflecting your child's love language may ease the transition. A calendar marking off the days passing before school starts can be a helpful way for children to keep track of school days approaching.

PHYSICAL TOUCH—Lots of cuddles and space to talk through going back to school can help; often just being listened to from the safety of caring arms is enough. Make a big generous hug part of getting out the door once shoes and coats are on.

WORDS OF AFFIRMATION—Remind your child of the things they enjoy about school and the qualities they have that get expressed there—"You're great at being friendly with other kids." "Math is your favorite subject; you can look forward to getting to do that again."

QUALITY TIME—Make sure the time your child will miss with you is made up for by some quality time at home. Find twenty minutes to sit and play with them, or get out a board game to enjoy together. This can be something to look forward to after the school day is finished.

RECEIVING GIFTS—Buy a new key ring for their backpack, some fun pens, or cool socks to mark going back to school.

ACTS OF SERVICE—Help your child prepare the items they need for school. This can be something you do together or something you get ready for them as a way of showing your love.

SPRING

Indoor, Outdoor, Seasons & Celebrations

Celebrating the change of seasons is a great way to mark the passing of the year and create a sense of family tradition. There are many signs that mark the passing of winter and coming of spring—longer days, warmer weather, the first buds or blossoms, birds returning, frogs in ponds. As a family, decide what your specific signs of spring are so you can celebrate the changing season.

PHYSICAL TOUCH—Get outdoors on a bright day to enjoy the sunshine on your skin. Find a bench where you can sit in the sun and enjoy some fresh air.

WORDS OF AFFIRMATION—Take a walk together and ask your child to describe the things that catch their eye. You can show you're really listening to your child by speaking back to them what they've just said. Talk about what you're looking forward to doing together with the change in weather.

QUALITY TIME—The important element to these activities to express Quality Time is that you give your child undivided attention, so put your phone on silent and dedicate your energy to this one moment.

RECEIVING GIFTS—Head out to choose and buy some seeds you can grow together, or buy a plant that will flower. You could try herbs that you'll be able to use as a family in your cooking, or just choose something you'll find beautiful or interesting to watch grow.

ACTS OF SERVICE—Have a spring clear out together: take time as a team to go through your child's room and work out what they no longer need so they're tidy and clear for the year ahead, or the next month at least!

SUMMER
Outdoor, Seasons & Celebrations

Summer is the perfect time for getting outdoors for family fun. It's amazing how refreshing it can be to go outside and step away from jobs and to-do lists even for ten minutes—try it and let yourself enjoy the moment as much as the kids do.

PHYSICAL TOUCH—Get to the park, take a blanket, enjoy relaxing in the fresh air with your kids, or let your body be an excellent climbing frame for them to scale! Snuggle up to cloud watch together or close your eyes and see if you can identify sounds.

WORDS OF AFFIRMATION—As you play, make sure you affirm your child with your words—both their actions and their skills. Start with telling them that you like spending time together and that you love them and are proud of them.

QUALITY TIME—Take a ball or Frisbee to the park and enjoy hanging out and being physical together. Find a local pick-your-own farm to go strawberry or raspberry picking together.

RECEIVING GIFTS—Visit a store that has outdoor sports equipment and let them choose something to try together. Buy a nature discovery kit or get them a collecting bag they can use while you're out.

ACTS OF SERVICE—Plan ahead and pack snacks, drinks, or lunch to take out with you. Take a trash bag with you and collect any litter you see to leave the area in a nicer state.

AUTUMN

Outdoor, Seasons & Celebrations

Leaves, leaves, leaves! Regardless of age, even big kids don't tire of kicking through a pile of autumn leaves. There are many ways to mark this change of season . . .

PHYSICAL TOUCH—You guessed it—go leaf kicking! Enter into the moment of fun and join with your kids and see their delight. Piles of leaves also offer a great chance for play fights and dramatic leaps, lots of opportunity for physical touch.

WORDS OF AFFIRMATION—As you mark a change of season, it's a great chance to take stock of the last few months. Take this time to tell your kid something you were proud of or impressed by that they did this summer.

QUALITY TIME—Head out to go leaf collecting! See how many different shapes, sizes, or colors you can find. Have some creative time when you get back, adding googly eyes to turn them into leaf creatures, and if you have paints you could add bright colors first.

RECEIVING GIFTS—Buy art supplies for your leaf painting activity, or chunky wax crayons to do leaf rubbings together.

ACTS OF SERVICE—Autumn is a great time of year to get out together and serve your local community. Find neighbors who need help clearing leaves and spread some kindness together.

WINTER
Indoor, Seasons & Celebrations

Winter can be cozy and warm, a chance to wrap up and snuggle and appreciate home after the chilly outdoors. The weather often naturally leads us to indoor activities, giving you an opportunity to create and celebrate some winter traditions.

PHYSICAL TOUCH—Wrap up in a blanket with your kids! This is a great chance to snuggle and enjoy being physically close. You can also meet their physical touch needs by making sure they're well bundled up when they go outside—a warm child is a happy child!

WORDS OF AFFIRMATION—Take time to ask your child what they like or dislike about winter. Listening to their thoughts and opinions gives them value. Try writing a story together that's set in winter and let their imagination rove.

QUALITY TIME—Immerse yourself in an indoor activity your child loves. It's a perfect time for board games, Legos, or puzzles—puzzles can often be found in abundance in thrift stores. Make a home hot chocolate café with your kids; choose server, chef, and customer roles and enjoy the fun together.

RECEIVING GIFTS—Go to an upscale shop and get the fixings for luxurious hot chocolates with marshmallows, cream, and sprinkles. Buy or even make a snuggly scarf to wrap your child up in your love.

ACTS OF SERVICE—Kids will get a real thrill helping out in your neighborhood, so take this chance to be the people who clear the snow from paths and doorsteps. Serving others in this way together is a great bonding experience. If you don't have snow, you could collect donations for homeless charities or check on elderly neighbors. A card from a child can mean everything to someone homebound.

SNOW DAY!

Outdoor, Physical, Seasons & Celebrations

Snow provides such a great opportunity for enjoying the simple, fun things in life! Somehow building a snowman, having a snowball fight, or going sledding never gets old.

PHYSICAL TOUCH—Take a sled ride together, huddle behind a shelter together while you prepare to spring a snowball ambush, or carry smaller kids home at the end of play when their legs are tired.

WORDS OF AFFIRMATION—Build up your child's confidence in their body by praising them as they run, roll heavy snowballs, or take aim at a target. The words you speak to them about their bodies will become the voice they hear as adults, so boost them for life right now.

QUALITY TIME—Sometimes it can be hard to say yes if we're busy, tired, and stressed, but think about this: your yes right now will keep open your relationship pathways as they get older too.

RECEIVING GIFTS—A new hat that keeps ears warm or some waterproof gloves to save chilly fingers from the snow will be a gift that keeps on giving all winter long.

ACTS OF SERVICE—When you get in from your snowy activities, let your child know that you'll clear up their outdoor gear for them to demonstrate your love and care.

GIVING THANKS
Everyday

An attitude of thankfulness or gratitude has really been in the spotlight recently, and for good reason. It can be easy to compare our lives and possessions to those around us—there will always be more we could wish to do or have, but there's plenty of research out there that tells us that having more and being happier don't equate. Even in tough times there is something we can find to be thankful for, whether it's a moment sitting in the sunshine, having clothes on our backs, or receiving kindness from someone. Here are some ways to cultivate thankfulness in your household.

PHYSICAL TOUCH—For someone who receives love by physical touch, your words will always go deeper if you are touching when you say them, so give your kid a hug or put a hand on their shoulder and tell them how much you love them and are proud of them.

WORDS OF AFFIRMATION—Tell your child why you are thankful for them and what they mean to your life.

QUALITY TIME—Try taking turns naming something you're thankful for when you sit down to eat together. Make sure each person has a turn and is well listened to, asking them more about the reason or feelings behind the situation, occasion, or person they're giving thanks for.

RECEIVING GIFTS—One great way of cultivating thankfulness is sharing from what you have. You could donate some of your belongings to a worthy cause or give to a food bank to help model generosity as part of this.

ACTS OF SERVICE—Serving others is a great way of showing thanks. Doing a task that relieves someone else's burden can be something you help your child practice for others or that you do for them.

VISITING FRIENDS & FAMILY

Seasons & Celebrations

It can be a real treat for kids to see friends and family; the change of a new environment is really stimulating and enriching. Whether this is a regular feature of your life or a rare occurrence, how you talk to and treat your child in front of others speaks volumes to them of how they are loved and valued by you.

PHYSICAL TOUCH—Make sure your child feels physically comfortable, especially if they are around new people or relatives they don't see often. If they need time close to you while they adjust to the situation, that's fine. Don't expect your child to hug or kiss people if they don't want to—see if they'll be happy with a fist bump, high five, or shoulder pat.

WORDS OF AFFIRMATION—We all have funny stories of what our kids have been up to, but telling these to an audience can undermine them, especially if your child is in the same space while the story is being told. Instead, tell a story of something brave or kind they've done and really boost their sense of self-worth.

QUALITY TIME—Make sure your child is still getting the attention they need from you, even if there's lots going on. Giving quality time to your child will help ensure the day goes much better, even if there are plenty of other activities available.

RECEIVING GIFTS—This is a great opportunity to help your kids practice giving gifts, whether it's as simple as getting them to present the flowers you've brought along with you or giving them advance warning so they can make a little gift, drawing, or card themselves.

ACTS OF SERVICE—Teach your child the value of being a helpful visitor, and make sure you tidy-up toys together or offer to help clear the table or do some kitchen tidying together to model how it looks to be a thoughtful guest.

HOSTING FRIENDS & FAMILY

Seasons & Celebrations

Having guests in your home is a great time to let your kids shine. You can create opportunities for them to practice hosting and enjoy sharing their space.

PHYSICAL TOUCH—Give your child time to adjust to new people being in their space if they need it. Let them stay close to you or hide behind your legs; give reassuring touch if it helps them feel safe.

WORDS OF AFFIRMATION—Help your child shine as a host by telling your guests good things about them: "Charlotte, would you like to show your grandparents to the table and you can serve the tasty cake you made?"

welcome

"Reuben, you made your room look really nice. Do you want to take your friends up to play?"

QUALITY TIME—Before the visit, ask your child what they'd like to do together. Help them feel involved and considered in the planning to give them the most satisfaction in what you do with your guests.

RECEIVING GIFTS—Help your children prepare small gifts for your visitors. If they're staying over, help your kids set these up in a special place for your guests to find.

ACTS OF SERVICE—Help your child prepare their space before they invite people into it. Help them tidy their room and find toys or activities they'd like to have out for your guests.

BEACH / BY THE WATER

Outdoor, Physical

Being by water is a simple pleasure for young children—whether you're lucky enough to have access to a beach or need to get more creative finding a local lake, river, fountain, stream, or splash park. Wading in the water, taking pails and shovels, beach balls, or little boats to float—the simple pleasures are big hits that are relished time and again.

PHYSICAL TOUCH—One thing that's guaranteed when you play by water is that you'll end up with soggy kids, and getting wrapped up in a towel and snuggled on a parent's lap is a treat for both of you.

WORDS OF AFFIRMATION—Encourage your child's bravery when the water is cold, or if they find something scary about it and take a step toward conquering a fear, let them know you believe in them and will cheer them on at whatever speed they're able to go.

QUALITY TIME—When your kid asks you to come and play, say YES! You might really want to read a book or chat with a friend, but make the most of these opportunities when they ask for your company.

RECEIVING GIFTS—Consider giving your child fun little gifts like bubbles, mini-boats, a wind spinner, pails, or watering cans.

ACTS OF SERVICE—Be prepared to get wet to have fun with your kids, and be prepared for everyone getting soggy and needing help to change into spare clothes.

NATURE / WILD SPACES

Outdoor, Physical

Children have an innate sense of mystery and exploration, and have a unique perspective—quite literally as their noses are closer to the ground than yours! Spending time in nature can be a very relaxing and mindful time for parents as well as children, whether it's your local park or community vegetable garden or you can access wilder spaces like forests or desert or swamp.

PHYSICAL TOUCH—Follow your kid's lead and do what they do: get low down in the dirt with them, and let your hands get mucky as you discover what your child sees, the way they see it.

WORDS OF AFFIRMATION—Be attentive to what your child observes. Encourage them in their curiosity.

QUALITY TIME—If there are other families or people nearby, make sure your attention remains on your child; your one-on-one attention will fill their love tank.

RECEIVING GIFTS—A simple spyglass, field notebook, or collecting tin are great little gift ideas for this adventure.

ACTS OF SERVICE—Be willing to do what your kid asks—for example, taking a hiking trail that might be a little more challenging. Tell them, "For you . . . sure!"

RAINY-DAY PUDDLES
Outdoor, Physical

We all know that kids will jump feet first into a fun experience, and splashing about in puddles is the perfect example. Preparation is the key here: if you're ready for the mess that follows you can get on with enjoying the moment in all its soaking glory!

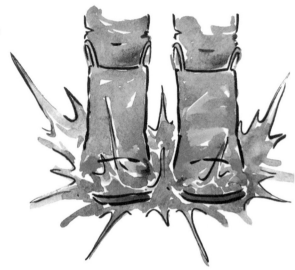

PHYSICAL TOUCH—The freedom and joy of splashing around in puddles will be wonderful for your child, and so too will be getting wrapped up in a dry, snuggly towel afterward to dry off and get warm.

WORDS OF AFFIRMATION—Encourage your child to really go for it. Give them full credit for how big they can splash and let them know you're enjoying them having this moment.

QUALITY TIME—Kids love it when their parents get fully involved in what they're doing, so pull on rain boots and join in the fun.

RECEIVING GIFTS—Now is the perfect time to present a new raincoat or umbrella. Letting your child know there's a hot chocolate waiting at home is also a great way to meet their Gifts love language.

ACTS OF SERVICE—Piles of soggy clothes? Let your child know you're clearing up the mess because you love them and wanted them to have the best time on this activity.

ANIMALS / FARMYARD

Outdoor

Most young children love interacting with animals, and a visit to a farm or zoo will be an exciting trip. A miniature farmyard in an urban park will work— even a trip to the pet store on a rainy day for little ones can be something to do! Sometimes a trip to a bigger attraction can be a bit overwhelming, so think beforehand about what would suit your child most. Will they be okay with not seeing everything if they like to take things in deeply and there's too much to see? Or if you know they're going to hate waiting in line for food or drinks, take supplies with you to eliminate this stress point.

PHYSICAL TOUCH—Smaller children may need picking up to see better—have a special moment with them as you do this. Older kids may want a pick-up too; otherwise, hold hands or have an arm around their shoulder while you look at something together.

WORDS OF AFFIRMATION—Watch out for ways your child is aware and helpful around others or acts kindly toward the animals, so you can compliment them.

QUALITY TIME—There'll be lots of photo opportunities on this visit, but make sure you also put your phone away to really absorb the moment together with your child.

RECEIVING GIFTS—We all know the phrase "exit through the gift shop." If a gift shop is in your budget, great! If not, take a small, related gift with you to avoid that tough moment for both you and your kid.

ACTS OF SERVICE—On a visit like this there are likely to be bags and layers of clothes discarded. Be prepared to show your love by carrying these items.

WHEELS, BIKES, SCOOTERS & BLADES
Outdoor

A trip out on wheels can be a great family activity—being in the fresh air always goes over well with kids and is a great way to burn off some energy. If your little ones are very small, you could try a bike trailer. Try a bike ride on quiet trails, scooting to the local park, or finding a kids' skate park to learn some new skills.

PHYSICAL TOUCH—Comfort any bumps, scrapes, or falls with big cuddles and reassurance. Give your child the safety of your arms until they feel ready to set off again.

WORDS OF AFFIRMATION—Encourage your child that they are strong and their body is capable. Give them confidence to keep going beyond what they think they can do.

QUALITY TIME—Instead of sitting on a bench to watch your kids play, find a way to join in with your kids, whether it's trotting alongside your little ones or finding wheels of your own so you can fully join in.

RECEIVING GIFTS—Try a bike bell or horn, handlebar tassels, stickers for their helmet, or a snack or drink that's a treat for the ride.

ACTS OF SERVICE—Help your child practice and improve their confidence and skills on one of the activities they're still learning.

SPORTS
Outdoor

Getting out for some sports can be a satisfying activity for everyone. You don't need to have just one activity; you can try out different options and see if any of them stick or have a variety of sports you know you like and can choose from. Make use of facilities in local parks and try out soccer, basketball, Frisbee, skateboarding, ping-pong, kite flying, or mini golf.

PHYSICAL TOUCH—Congratulate successes with high fives, chest bumps, a pat on the back, or an arm around the shoulder.

WORDS OF AFFIRMATION—When you're trying new activities, offer lots of encouragement and positive energy, especially if your children are finding it tricky—it's a great opportunity for growing in perseverance.

QUALITY TIME—Your time together is a given here! Sample different activities to find something that you and your child both love and will hopefully want to come back to again and again.

RECEIVING GIFTS—Any new sports equipment makes a great gift, or secretly bring one of their favorite treats to surprise them with when you take a break.

ACTS OF SERVICE—Make time to help your child get some practice in at home.

GARDENING/GROWING
Outdoor

There's something so exciting about seeing little shoots emerge from seeds you've sown—you don't need heaps of space to enjoy a little bit of gardening with your child. If you want a quick result, try cress or other salad leaves; otherwise let the kids choose what inspires them (just check the information on the seed packet to ensure that what they've chosen will work for your environment).

PHYSICAL TOUCH—Sowing seeds is a very tactile activity, so make sure your kids can make a bit of a mess and enjoy getting soil on their hands and watering. When you help them get clean afterward, help them get up to the sink and take time washing their hands.

WORDS OF AFFIRMATION—Step back and let your child be hands-on; tell them what a great job they're doing making new life grow and taking care of the seeds.

QUALITY TIME—Head to the local store to buy seeds together. Take time to look at all the choices and enjoy spotting plants that look interesting on the seed packets.

RECEIVING GIFTS—Give your child a budget to buy seeds and money for the shop so they can enjoy the satisfaction of buying something they're going to use.

ACTS OF SERVICE—Okay, this activity may get messy. Take time to set up so you can be relaxed and enjoy the moment while dirt is being spilled, and cleaning up later becomes a way of serving your child.

DOG WALK
Outdoor, Physical

If you don't have your own pet dog, then borrowing a dog will be a fun activity for your kid. If you don't know a friendly neighbor or family member who can lend you a pooch, try a dog borrowing website to find someone local who is happy for their dog to be taken out.

PHYSICAL TOUCH—Getting to pet a friendly doggy is a tactile treat for most children. You can join in and show your child which types of touch will be most liked.

WORDS OF AFFIRMATION—When you see your child being kind, caring, gentle, responsible, or thoughtful, name these attributes and tell them how proud you are of them.

QUALITY TIME—Taking time to do this activity is expressing love to your child; make sure you can give your full attention to your child while you're out.

RECEIVING GIFTS—Take a photo to remember the occasion and print it out so your child can put it somewhere they'll see it often. If it's okay with the dog's owner, get some treats your child can give to the dog.

ACTS OF SERVICE—Spend time teaching your child how to care for the dog and groom it together. Research this together if it's also new to you.

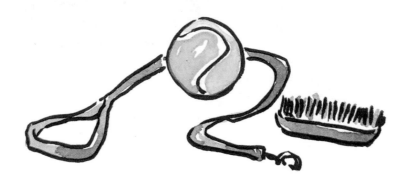

LIBRARY

Indoor, Creative

Visiting the library is a great free resource and a way of helping your child explore the world.

PHYSICAL TOUCH—Sit your child on your lap or sit shoulder to shoulder to flip through books together before you decide what to borrow.

WORDS OF AFFIRMATION—Show your children how to take care of books and compliment them anytime you see them doing this. Although you might know which sorts of books your child is most likely to enjoy, also encourage them to try other possibilities and make room for unexpected choices. You never know what interests might get activated in them.

QUALITY TIME—Make sure you have enough time so you don't have to rush. If you're taking more than one child, take care to spend time with each, looking at what they're choosing and listening to what they're thinking.

RECEIVING GIFTS—There's great freedom to borrowing books, but one you can keep is also very special. Each library visit put a little money in a fund that they know will be for buying a book in the future.

ACTS OF SERVICE—Who wants to carry books? Carry your kids' books and let them know you're doing it because you love them.

STORYBOOK WRITING

Indoor, Creative

Your children have fascinating imaginations, and writing a story together will create space for you to see more of their innate personality. Depending on age, this will be anything from your kids adding squiggly doodles to the story you write down to it being written and drawn without any hands-on help from you at all. Create a booklet from loose sheets of paper stapled or stuck together and invite your children to work with you to create their own personalized story or adventure— it can include anything they can dream up! Think of yourself as helping to draw little mysteries out of them.

PHYSICAL TOUCH—Little children can sit on your lap to tell you their ideas or add their drawings. Scooch down close, next to kids who are creating their own books, touching their shoulder while you look at what they're making.

WORDS OF AFFIRMATION—Compliment their work, whether it be the ideas they're thinking of, the effort they're putting into drawing or writing, or just letting them know you enjoy hearing their ideas.

QUALITY TIME—Create a clear space to work together so they know they're in a special zone with you.

RECEIVING GIFTS—Present tools of the trade in a box or gift bag before you tell them what the plan is as a teaser to this activity. (Of course, they might come up with a completely different idea, so be prepared to pivot!)

ACTS OF SERVICE—Help your child find the stationery and supplies they want to use for this project.

FORT BUILDING

Indoor, Creative, Physical

Kids love creating special places where their imaginations can run wild, and this is why fort building will never get old. Bringing some new construction materials along will add new interest, so grab blankets, pillows, cardboard boxes, chairs, pegs, and duvets and get creating!

PHYSICAL TOUCH—The likelihood is you'll be squeezed into a little spot together, so physical touch is a given. If you get climbed on in the process, all the better.

WORDS OF AFFIRMATION—Be encouraging about the construction ideas your child has, and if they don't work, help them to try new options.

QUALITY TIME—Many a magical memory has been made in a play fort, so get involved, listen to your child, and see how lovely it can be stepping back into this childhood activity.

RECEIVING GIFTS—Go all out for the castle theme and create some cardboard crowns to present to your children to decorate (think cereal boxes and felt-tip pens). Create one for yourself as well and see if they'd like to decorate yours for you.

ACTS OF SERVICE—It's also a lot of fun when the fort falls apart and gets demolished, so stick around for this part and work as a family team to tidy-up. Even introduce a supply chain to put things back if you have enough people.

DANCE PARTY

Indoor, Creative, Physical

A great way to blow off some steam and have some fun together is to put on some tunes and dance around your home. There may well be music your kids already know and love from films or school, but it can also be fun to share some of your own personality by introducing your favorite music.

PHYSICAL TOUCH—Smaller kids love being carried or spun around while you dance. You can also teach your kids new moves, high-five each other, or even experiment with some ballroom dancing and do a duet together.

WORDS OF AFFIRMATION—Compliment your kids' moves and energy and tell them how you enjoy spending time with them.

QUALITY TIME—Make a playlist that lasts twenty minutes or more and you can forget about the clock and put all your energy into enjoying dancing with your kid.

RECEIVING GIFTS—This is a great time to indulge in some silly fun. Find some sequin clothes for disco dancing, tutus to dance some ballet, or face paints to rock it out!

ACTS OF SERVICE—Yes, your kids may love music that isn't your top choice; love them by indulging their current tastes!

DRESS-UP & MAKE-BELIEVE
Indoor, Creative

Before there were Disney costumes there were boxes of scarves, shoes, hats, and waistcoats for dressing up. Collect an eclectic mystery box of items (think thrift shop or back-of-wardrobe treasures) and bring it out on a rainy or wintry day. Let the kids hunt through the box for what catches their eye and have fun creating characters for the outfits they make. If they need something to do, have a tea party or go on an imaginary adventure together in their new outfits.

PHYSICAL TOUCH—Help your children change into the new clothes or help them adapt the items they've got for how they want to wear them.

WORDS OF AFFIRMATION—Affirm your child's creativity and ideas and let them know you're enjoying playing with them and spending time together.

QUALITY TIME—You may have other jobs that need your attention, but twenty minutes' undistracted play with your child will really fill their love tank.

RECEIVING GIFTS—Anytime you find a new item for the box, pop it in a gift bag and make an occasion of it.

ACTS OF SERVICE—Give your child help creating their outfit; find extra items or help them adjust their clothes until they're satisfied.

IMAGINARY VACATION

Indoor, Creative

Kids love the idea of being on
vacation, often way more than
in real life! But giving kids an
experience in their imagination
can carry a lot of the satisfaction
of the real thing, for a lot less effort
and cost. So, when you're at loose
ends or stuck inside, try an imaginary
vacation. Ask your kids where they'd like to go (go
with whatever wacky ideas they have), pack some little bags, and
set off on your make-believe adventure.

TICKET
magic carpet
ride to
THE MOON

PHYSICAL TOUCH—However you travel to your "destination," get
close in your boat/plane/train/carriage/magic carpet. Add some fun
to the journey by providing bumps and fast corners as you squish
together on cushions, in a box, or under a table.

WORDS OF AFFIRMATION—Really listen to all the ideas your kid has and speak them back to your child with curiosity and an attitude of being impressed. They'll love the attention their ideas are getting.

QUALITY TIME—Being present in this mini-adventure may well create a memory that lasts, so get in the moment and let yourself relax and be in holiday mode!

RECEIVING GIFTS—All parents know that snacks make an essential element to journeys for kids, so even if you just break out a box of crackers at an opportune moment, food for the journey is a great gift.

ACTS OF SERVICE—Of course, there's a good chance this is going to create some mess. So your act of service is cleaning up after the adventure (and it may just prove quicker and easier if you do it yourself!).

JUNK SCULPTURES

Indoor, Creative

Kids love being experimental and creative, and this one is an easy win to get out when you're lacking ideas or stuck inside in bad weather. Collect all your waste packaging in a big container—think cereal boxes, toilet rolls, plastic bottle lids, egg cartons—and have a few extras like pipe cleaners and googly eyes, along with some glue sticks and tape. The aim? Whatever your kid feels like making—maybe a sculpture, monster, vehicle, or a home for their favorite toy.

PHYSICAL TOUCH—Help your child with tricky tasks and you'll be right beside them, or have your arms around them as you help them assemble their vision.

WORDS OF AFFIRMATION—Refrain from pointing out what you think might be a better way to do something. Instead, compliment the choices they're making and the ideas they have.

QUALITY TIME—Depending on how long they want to create, you may not spend the entire time joining in with this one, but it is important that, when they want to show you what they've made or ask for your help, you give them your undivided attention. Make sure you make eye contact when they show you something and get physically close to where they are. Your physical presence lets them know your attention is fully with them.

RECEIVING GIFTS—Buy some crafty extras as a gift for this activity—ribbons, craft printed paper, feathers—whatever your kids would enjoy using.

ACTS OF SERVICE—Be your child's assistant, helping them achieve their vision by applying staples, scotch tape, and stickers as directed!

HOME DINING

Indoor, Creative, Everyday

This is a real-life version of a "kids café" game. Children love the opportunity to prepare and serve food, and you can have lots of fun creating your own home restaurant that indulges the things that most interest them. Maybe they want to help prepare the food; serving it might be their highlight, or creating a beautiful table, or drawing a menu you can order from. This is great for a busy or wet day, as you can set them off on the preparations and also enjoy your time together when you eat.

PHYSICAL TOUCH—Help your children wash and dry their hands, demonstrate food preparation in a hands-on way, or be a silly customer and pretend to sit down on the same chair as your child and enjoy the giggles that follow.

WORDS OF AFFIRMATION—Compliment your child on the effort they've put into preparing food, creating menus, setting the table, or serving you.

QUALITY TIME—Make sure there's a time during this activity where your kid gets your full attention; sitting to eat together is the prime example.

RECEIVING GIFTS—Maybe your child would love their own aprons or chef's hats, or maybe you could get out some special cups and plates they can use for their café.

ACTS OF SERVICE—Help your children with the setup of their game and help them find the items they need for their ideas.

MUSIC MAKING
Indoor, Creative

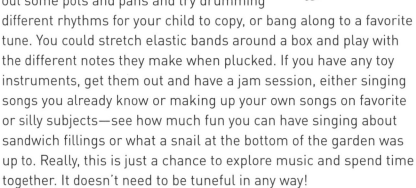

First of all, if you don't consider yourself to be musical—don't panic! We're not looking for musical perfection here, just some fun and experimentation that allows your child to explore and play. You could get out some pots and pans and try drumming different rhythms for your child to copy, or bang along to a favorite tune. You could stretch elastic bands around a box and play with the different notes they make when plucked. If you have any toy instruments, get them out and have a jam session, either singing songs you already know or making up your own songs on favorite or silly subjects—see how much fun you can have singing about sandwich fillings or what a snail at the bottom of the garden was up to. Really, this is just a chance to explore music and spend time together. It doesn't need to be tuneful in any way!

PHYSICAL TOUCH—Hold your child as you demonstrate ways to play different instruments or tap out a rhythm on their leg.

WORDS OF AFFIRMATION—Give your child positive guidance on different ways they can play an instrument or the sounds they can make.

QUALITY TIME—Roll up your sleeves and make some noise. Your child will be delighted with your participation as you connect over music.

RECEIVING GIFTS—Little gifts can be wonderful treats, especially when wrapped up. Try plastic pots filled with beans to make shakers, a box and a variety of elastic bands to make a "guitar," or some castanets.

ACTS OF SERVICE—Join in the way your child asks you to. If you're asked to whistle their favorite movie soundtrack on repeat, so be it!

BODY MOVEMENT

Indoor, Physical

Dance and body movement can be a fun way for kids to engage with physical activity. You might feel confident enough to set this up and lead it with your kids, but if not there's a wealth of YouTube channels brimming with fun ways to be physically active with your kids, often with stories intertwined to keep them in the moment. Look for children's dance or activity videos. Experiment to see what works best for you.

PHYSICAL TOUCH—Help your child into moves and positions with gentle, guiding hands.

WORDS OF AFFIRMATION—Encourage your child to try things they find tricky and praise their efforts, regardless of how "right" they're getting the actions.

QUALITY TIME—Join in with your kids and be prepared to be a "beginner" again.

RECEIVING GIFTS—Give them a new water bottle, a funky headband, or exercise clothes.

ACTS OF SERVICE—Help your child practice tricky moves or create space in your home for them to expend all their physical energy.

OBSTACLE COURSE

Indoor, Physical

This is a great rainy-day activity and can be done using whatever you have around you at home. Create an obstacle course using chairs and cushions, going under tables, over beds, and behind sofas. Your kids will love setting this up with you, so even if the course itself doesn't take very long, you'll still get plenty of time together, and you may well find they want to keep going when you think you've finished!

PHYSICAL TOUCH—Add body obstacles like going through your legs or having a donkey ride on your back for part of the course.

WORDS OF AFFIRMATION—Encourage your child's ideas for the course and cheer them on when they're taking their turn.

QUALITY TIME—Make sure you watch their efforts as they take their turn. Giving your child your undistracted gaze is significant and meaningful.

RECEIVING GIFTS—Find a little treat as a finishing prize for the course.

ACTS OF SERVICE—Spend time setting up the course for your child to enjoy or work with them to create the course they want to build.

TREASURE HUNT

Indoor, Outdoor, Physical

This one is great for a rainy or wintry day, or to get kids out into the yard, and can be done at any age level—whether you draw simple pictures for little ones, do a little covert reading practice for new learners, or write riddles as clues for bigger kids. Hide a favorite toy and make it into a rescue mission by following the clues, or wrap up a little gift like a new notepad or book to find at the end. Just draw or write a series of clues for anywhere in your home you're happy for them to go and let the fun ensue!

PHYSICAL TOUCH—Congratulate the treasure finders with big hugs or high fives.

WORDS OF AFFIRMATION—Encourage them to keep going when they're losing motivation and cheer them on when they have success.

QUALITY TIME—Some kids will definitely want you along for the hunt; others will want to tell you all about it when they're done, so make sure you give them space and time to tell you about their experience.

RECEIVING GIFTS—Make the treasure they seek a little gift, and it will bring a whole new energy to your treasure hunt!

ACTS OF SERVICE—Your work and preparation setting up the hunt is Acts of Service being expressed.

SCHOOL & HOMEWORK

Everyday

At some point, you're going to be negotiating homework with your kids. Here are some ways to bring the love languages into the mix and help ease the process for you and your child.

PHYSICAL TOUCH—Let little ones sit on your knee or cozy up next to you to read. With bigger kids sitting at a table to work, stop with an arm over their shoulder to see how they're doing.

WORDS OF AFFIRMATION—Help your child have faith in themselves with challenging work. Make sure you listen to and acknowledge their feelings, and then let them know you believe in them and encourage them to keep going.

QUALITY TIME—Set out a clear reward of Quality Time with you in a way your child loves for after they've completed their task. Find something you can do sitting next to them to keep them company while they work.

RECEIVING GIFTS—Buy some new pens or notebooks to inspire and energize your child with their homework.

ACTS OF SERVICE—When your child is struggling with a task, come alongside them and help them work their way through it.

THEATER & PERFORMANCES

Creative

Seeing a show on stage is a real treat, whether you're at a theater or watching street performers. Make sure you find something a suitable length for your child's attention span. If a full theater trip is too much of a stretch, see if you can

catch a musical rehearsal in a public space that you can join and leave at any time. During school breaks there may be free local performances to find, so you can try things out and see what your child likes before committing to a full show.

PHYSICAL TOUCH—Put an arm around your child's shoulder as you watch the show, sit them on your lap, or lift them up to make sure they can see everything.

WORDS OF AFFIRMATION—Seeing a show is likely to inspire some repeat performances in your children, so make sure you encourage and support them flexing their performance muscles.

QUALITY TIME—Being together is a given for this activity; make sure you have plenty of time to get to the show and enjoy the atmosphere so you're not rushing through anything.

RECEIVING GIFTS—Wrap up the tickets and surprise your child with them as an unexpected gift.

ACTS OF SERVICE—Help your child prepare to go out by choosing an outfit together and letting them join in with some of the grown-up ways you get ready, like a little perfume/aftershave or a special hair style.

FLASHLIGHT WALK
Outdoor, Physical

Nighttime and darkness can be a magical adventure for kids, something they don't experience very often. Taking your kids for a nighttime exploration can be a fun and unusual activity that they'll remember long afterward. Certain times of year may be easier to do this, but a dawn, dusk, sunrise, or sunset walk is also a special time of day if you need another option. Chasing and jumping onto spots of light from a flashlight can motivate weary legs to keep going.

PHYSICAL TOUCH—Hold hands as you explore, especially if the dark has a scary edge for small children.

WORDS OF AFFIRMATION—Give your child your reassurance that they're safe with you. Make sure you're listening to the particular things your child notices and let them know you're paying attention to their observations.

QUALITY TIME—Let your child know this is a special activity and adventure you're taking together, and you're doing it because you want to spend time with them.

RECEIVING GIFTS—Little flashlights are the perfect gift for this activity.

ACTS OF SERVICE—Taking care of your child as you're out on this exciting-scary activity expresses Acts of Service.

LITTER CLEANUP
Outdoor, Physical

Heading out into your local streets or a favorite park to pick up litter is a great way of giving back to your community, and your kids will be energized by doing something that has a noticeable impact and benefits others. Make sure you're equipped with strong refuse sacks, protective gloves, and hand wipes or sanitizer. Little ones can always be litter spotters, sending you to swoop in on the offending trash.

PHYSICAL TOUCH—Have a team huddle at the start of your pick, with your arms around their shoulders as you go over your plan.

WORDS OF AFFIRMATION—Have a conversation with your child about what impact your actions will have on others and ask how it makes them feel. Let them know you're proud of them for doing something for the community.

QUALITY TIME—Sometimes the best time for conversations with your child is while you are doing an activity, so make sure you leave enough pauses for your child to bring up anything they want to talk about.

RECEIVING GIFTS—Ever seen how excited kids get about using one of those "claw" litter pickers? One of these will add a surprising amount of energy to your efforts!

ACTS OF SERVICE—In this activity you are helping your child experience what it's like to love others through an act of service.

FAMILY WALKS
Outdoor, Physical, Everyday

We all know going for a family walk can sometimes become a painful and exhausting process, so here are a variety of ideas to keep your children busy and interested so everyone can enjoy the walk and get all the way around! Make your children "walk leaders," and where possible, let them choose the route. Or get them to leave signs on the path as a code trail for you to follow. Set a scavenger hunt for your kids—a rainbow challenge to find every color of flower or as many different leaf shapes as possible, or record how many types of bugs they can find. Take treats for en route: a thermos of hot chocolate, some baked goods to have on a bench, or a picnic blanket and packed lunch. Take turns running ahead and hiding to surprise the rest of the group. To help children catch up, give them a shouted count-out to see how quickly they can reach you.

PHYSICAL TOUCH—Swing small children up in the air between two adults, or give a little piggyback or shoulder ride to kids with weary legs.

WORDS OF AFFIRMATION—Encourage your child's sense of achievement by pointing out how far they've come under the power of their own two little legs.

QUALITY TIME—Be attentive to what draws your kids' attention and be their partner as they explore and follow their curiosity.

RECEIVING GIFTS—Try a small rucksack to encourage independence, new comfy walking socks, or a little camera so they can take photos of your adventures.

ACTS OF SERVICE—Even with all these ideas kids may well get weary legs, so prepare some snacks for a stop en route and consider giving little carries to reenergize a tired child.

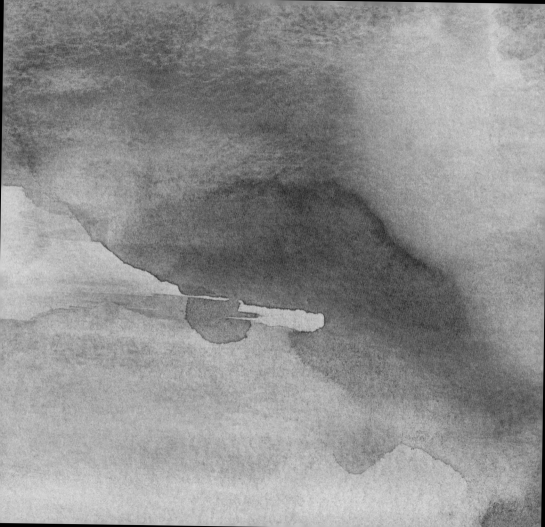